# APOCRYPHA

## Early Collected Poems

Colin Dardis

First Edition: 2022
Rs. 200/-

**Cyberwit.net**
HIG 45 Kaushambi Kunj, Kalindipuram
Allahabad - 211011 (U.P.) India
http://www.cyberwit.net
Tel: +(91) 9415091004
E-mail: info@cyberwit.net



Printed at VCORE CONNECT LLP.

# Contents

# To Speak of Donegal

To speak of the sunset
in postcard terms
would be falsehood;
injustice in saying
*radiant*
or *bedazzling*.

Rather, a lie of pink
washed over a tarpaulin sea,
the tide as wild
as a hot white flash of magnesium
or the curl of her hair
across the bathroom floor;
each contour of wave
reflecting the bend of eyelash
she wore on palatable skin.

With this stretch of sand
teased into the bay,
woven between rock and knot
and the names we carved
disappearing with our steps,
our sun, our tide,
yet indelible on our hearts.

# Visions of Atlantic

We wrestled a path
up a Donegal mountain face
and sneaked our way
into an Atlantic view
full of grandeur and sparkle,
with walnut brown crags
domineering Northern waves
as they charged forth:
crash of wildebeest,
each trashing pure, white froth
into unmoving cliffs.
The ocean stretched out around us,
dipping beyond the horizon,
awaiting sunset,
with Tory Island peeking down
through the cloud
at the smalt blue coastline.
It was mid-Autumn,
with the tarred front of cloud
only lifting that morning.
The wind was still cruel,
but that sight, that shimmering
clear, frozen sight,
demanded us to stay.

# Deepest Breath

Wild calls of abandonment
comes rushing down the mountain
in the guise of mist and rain,

the cover of winter invites adventure,
a test of the elements against
the temperament of man.

Carry yourself across the crags,
the land-crashed hills, earthen downs,
come trail through skyland and cloud

to Heaven's peak, where God will whisper
the secrets of life to those that brave
the blind summit of today.

Here is your deepest breath,
all affirmation comes,
interwoven with passion and privilege.

The fire of achievement burns away
season's frost, us, one more step
along our kindling journey.

# A Persistent Wind

Brought the car down
to the mountain foot.
It was a day full of minor chords:
clouds layered with arpeggios
and a six-string wind
pushed the mist in,
packing it tight around the coast
like crushed cotton.
We lay under staccato rain
and waited:
waves kept rolling,
but the weather remained,
demonstrating nature's tenacity
for denying vernal pleasures.

We did not care
for choral showers or baritone skies.
We took our car
and drove back to the hotel;
one room, two lovers
and the freedom of warm sheets.

# Belfast Drinks Up and Goes Home

Belfast
will drink up and go home,
as soon as it has finished
beating down on its neighbour.

Belfast
will be drinking up and heading home
just as soon as it finishes
pissing behind this barstool.

Belfast
is just about to down its pint and head on home,
after blowing its taxi fare
on the grease-ridden slot machine in the corner.

Belfast
will momentarily slurp the dregs and head out the door
but only after making a horrendous pass
at Antrim's girl.

Belfast
drinks up and goes home
only to find that no one cares to remember
where its home is.

# Let's Wrestle

I've been pinned
straight in the middle of the ring,
1, 2, 3,
and still I'm kicking against the bell,
refusing to listen to the count.
The crowd has gone home,
the referee has wiped off the blood
and the cameras have been switched off;
but still I'm fighting on,
stomping on my shadow,
waiting for our rematch.

# Superhero

I would be powered by sadness,
an infinite vein
standing long and blue
on the arm of humanity.

# Songbird

They say a caged bird
will always sing
for want of being
free.
Imagine if
there was no sight
to behold
beyond those bars
but brick walls
insulating metal rails,
no sky
to line dreams,
with darkness
calling out
to be a friend.
What song
would the bird
sing then?

# Another Nail in the Old Wooden Coffin

There are always words to entertain us,
that pageantry of language
stringing moments and events together,
a tapestry of time and recollection
where tradition and modernism meet.

I'll learn another word, another poem,
become another strangled actor
trying to make it to the second act,
frantically looking across the theatre
for any sign of an interval.

The play continues; I pluck
another nail out from my coffin,
hammer down my makeshift stage.
I'll rip these boards up,
only to be buried in them again.

# As Seen On TV

You don't look good,
despite the diet pills
and new dress.

Yes, black is supposed to be slimming,
and yes, I'm supposed to smile
and tell you all the lovely
chocolate-coated persiflage
that should drip easily out of friends' mouths
but the words that find my tongue
are not melliferous;
they are wrapped with the cold, dawning barbs of truth.

So reach for the coal sack,
the paper bag, the nurses' screen:
you are not glamorous in your presentation,
but God bless you for trying.
Yet you are prettier
than the ugly mouth I carry round
flattening your desires.

# On Mistakes In Drawings

I make my drawings
in pen, permanent marker;
no HB graphite shit for me,
that's stuff for the fakers
and the patient.

I draw fast,
lopping arcs of pendulum ink
swing across the page.
More often than not,
a line goes out of orbit
and I cannot erase.

You work with your mistakes,
blend them into the whole,
another word in the silent poetry.

If art reflects life
then there should be no chances
for corrections.
Hold the artist accountable
and let the canvas be their guilt.

# Please Return This Poem

If lost, please return this poem
to the initial thought that spurred it,
the big bang moment
of one synapse igniting
a forest of the brain,
fuelled by the oxygen of beauty,
humanity's greatest inspiration.

If lost, return this poem
to a patch of Ireland
resting by the motorway of creation,
away from industrial exhausts
and mankind measured in fiscal terms,
back to the moment of tranquillity
that gave forth its seed
to germinate in art's heavy bosom.

If lost, return this poem
to the soul's waiting room
in hope that beauty is found again,
replicated by divine practices
so that the beholder may press
their inked offspring to the world.

# Black Lines Across the Countryside

Amongst the dew heavy moss
and wildflower,
someone perched a weather station,
as if technology
could ever co-exist
with grass and rock.

We tumbled over a broken fence,
only to find a disused quarry
with no way down.
Turning back,
I traced telegraph poles
and electric cable
through fields and mountains,
imagining that whoever built
these deluded monuments
must have imagined he was hoisting up
God's own great washing line.

# A Schoolbag Full Of Rocks

This schoolbag heaves
with unread books:
tomes for learning, for display,
for keeps.
Nine years old,
carrying his father's
*Introduction*
*to  Philosophy.*
It is a word that suggests
nobility, prestige,
the accomplishment of education.

This book,
the philosophy tome,
is no playground ammunition:
it does not impress friends,
conquer the taunt of bullies
or attract girls.

It is for
teacher's admiration
only,
the quiet wonder
of children
and their efforts.

# Perhaps

Perhaps a string of kisses would drape
the tender nape
of your stretching neck
framed within
an auburn pillow;
perhaps we could turn to yellow
in this crystal sunrise,
a golden nest around our bed
praising the wisdom
of our slumber;
perhaps the world will thunder
to arouse
this pellucid girl and boy;
caught adrift their morning love:
the deep embrace of each other;
perhaps they could be lovers.

# Candlestick

This candle was not made for church,
nor cake nor celebration.

It is to be used in voids of light
with the flame echoing off vacant walls,
filling rooms with the volume of luminescence.

A spotlight for the late night
reader or scribe, a friend to call upon
in the abandonment of daylight,
knowing a romance beyond
the electric torch or kerosene lamp.

Used sparingly, or lit through long winter hours,
a silver teardrop still shines from its mountaintop.

Eventually, it will melt and whither
until only a stump of once proud trunk remains,
a burnt thread of a wick
peeking through the wax,
still asking for the flame.

# Watermelon

Some talk of a seed of love:
it could be deciphered
from the sugar juice
that drips from your lip
that one sacrificed love
for gluttony instead.

If you could have kept
that slice in tact
then I would have loved those lips
like your tongue loved spooning
that fruit syrup
into your greedy mouth.

And I would have loved
to have been a seed
caught within that moment of time,
like an orchid's expanse of petal
unfolding into a delicatessen
of desire.

# A Steady Progression

These vagabond streets have been dried out:
bloodless, silent; a sorrowful vacuum
without alignment of mourners
to allow dignity in passing.

All business: each brick laid
with the acumen of progress;
life more privy to reallocation
than happily abandonment.

The telephone wires sprawl
across charted dead tarmac,
cut in the astute knowledge
that no mouth moves in prayer here.

# Kissing an Eel

Boil her lips
and let the flesh congeal,
skim off the skin and see
what a meal this makes.

Physically defective,
kissing an eel.
How does it feel to kiss this eel?

Black and slime,
wet coal,
a clump of turf
soaked by the rains of Ireland;
pressing your tongue into a dark bog land

with your lack of emotion
portrayed in a Tupperware heart.

# A Perfect Circle

The road out of this town
is elusive: a dirt track
through bog and marshland,
a meadow path, a cobblestone street
twisting and meandering river
forming banks from broken earth,
searching for a path to flow.

I followed the water,
hoping not to find a delta
or the mouth of the bay,
but for captured rain to turn
into itself, creating
a perfect circle,
a circle of distance, of indifference
to take me out of this town
and afford me a variant of viewpoint.

# There is nothing

there is nothing
there is silence
and that is something

there is a void
but there is a place
in which the void exists
and that is something

there is something
that forms the shell
to hold the gap
that creates the void
so there *is* something
within the four walls
that creates the ever
reverberating echo
that reminds us
of the void

it is the cry
of the lovelorn
and wantless

and that is something

# For All the Silent Nights

For all the silent nights, uninterrupted
by the calls of abandoned lovers,
for all the dead air breathed
without a wave to crack its fragility,
for all the forgotten words
left to find their autumn,
for all the catalogued dreams
that will never know our touch,
for all the whispered prayers
trapped underneath the bed sheets,
for all the empty arms
falling asleep, unfulfilled,
you did not cry.

# Tested

There is no thrill in the assured victory,
Lady Fate cradling your path in her palms:
the fight, the struggle, tactics and stratagems,
that's where the game lies, wrapped up not in silk,
but in blood-stained cotton, knowing mud and sweat,
soil and toil. Whether you be best or bested,
to be tested is a triumph for all.

The squash match is a jaded contest,
for muscles that know nothing of exertion
will not grow in strength; the unchallenged force
will not gain in character; the pugilist
sparring below their weight class deserves
neither their place in podium nor ring.

## Seaweed and Moss

On a small beach,
the smallest of Ireland perhaps:

feet of sand
as taut as skin of drum.
unbroken by foot;

black brick of coastal rock,
all seaweed and moss;

weight of tick-tock waves,
pendulum water collapsing
over itself; candy floss curl,
fold of cake mix slide;

tugboat tide, no respite,
unrelenting lunar drag
pulling oceans in.

Sit, give way
to this distinct splendour
of simple repetition;
history will not record this moment,
yet it is still mine to be remembered.

# A Civic Reflux

A twitching, quivering stream
of secretion scintillates
weary, oppidan senses:

the thick new blood of a butcher's display
standing cold and outright
in its unabashed raw glory;
cigarette ash flittering
as charred butterfly wings;
restaurants failing to mimic
homely scents of mother's roast dinner;
a beggar's growl
beneath stale, tired clothes;
the hunger of charity
in wet copper coins;
scenes of rust and concrete
in every urban corner.

Your mind searches for
grass, air, a river,
finding only a reflux of tyres,
chalk, grit and coffee.

No pearl is formed
from collecting these expulsions,
expectorating the mere essences
of ourselves.

# Homeless

I use to live in seventy-two: it's bricked up now though
in the way of anonymity that these terraces
seem to succumb to; when a house becomes a home, it's cause
to celebrate with the tradition of bringing forth warmth
to the smiling new residents resplendent in their snug,
regardless of responsibility, mortgages, risk;
but when a home becomes a house, there's no ceremony,
simply handymen busy with their mortar and chipboard
plugging those telling holes of dead doors and wilted windows.
There is nothing left to hold the legend of families
once inhabiting now redundant shells, void of value,
just the neglect that weeds enjoy and graffiti'd thresholds
bearing down on abandoned streets, populised only by
the stray dogs that know of no place to rest from the downfall.

# Bring It Down Gently

Her morning expanse glides into place
between my duvet and my body.
These sheets will go four weeks unwashed;
clinging to her presence, sweat beads soaked
into fibres, her curvature still silhouetted
in the linen. A delicious memory of one long hair
draped over the headboard: it hangs there,
at peace, for four days, as dreams of her
fall over my pillow.
                    Eventually, the hair
slides down to the carpet, mixes in with the fluff.
I will wash the sheets after the cold realisation
that it is my sweat, my hair, my dirt I sleep in,
and find another memento to cleave to instead.

# The Stare From Across The Room

Nine years past,
according to the newspaper,
and still he has kept that doll:
same chair, same corner,
despite the damp.

His wife's wedding dress
as a cushion,
although you would have thought
the rear was soft enough
for composure.

He never made mention
to any house-callers,
and all were wise
not to hold their eyes for too long
across the crude stitching.

It was course and ragged
and as stuffed with age as Jim was,
old mottled reminder
of companionship,
long dead but never buried.

# Dualism

With a Cartesian knife
I detach your mind from your body
and only yearn for one;
unable to tell which is the better half,
tonight I am unsure.

On previous days,
I thought with my mind
and wanted yours to rub against,
expected the resulting friction
to fire off creative sparks.

Or I ran with my body
and sought out your flesh;
this experiment was as much
an examination of my own skin
as it was of yours.

Right now,
I feel there will never be a union,
as my mind and body
will not allow
us to come together.

# Flagging

Crouch under the flag parade,
countenance slung on your houses
with the pride of the homeowner
in council estates and rented slums.

Collect the bunting from the attic,
borrow the neighbour's ladder
for this annual regime, streaked
through years of habitation.

Touch up those murals, lads,
the weather gods must listen
to prayers from the other side,
a hoped-for erosion sent.

And sure, the wind soon wraps
the flags tightly around the poles
like failed candyfloss, unreadable
yet intention clear by geography.

# Night of No Choices

In the night of no choices,
when the roads are closed by myriads
of floods and concrete,
when the roof of the sky
has been lowered so
that the clouds ball up in your throat
and all the rivers are impassable,
your feet broken by their glass banks,
turn, turn against the poisoned air
and traverse the pathways of yourself,
finding new archways and tunnels
to shelter under.
                    Your wings have not
felt the oil slick of The Depression,
do not think your feathers too greasy
to bat away the rain with.
                    Your soul
is still a tower, welcoming to
every avenue of your indestructible age.

# Trashlined

Dead dregs of pockets,
useless coppers and loose threads
in faded jeans, hanging from
the great rumble of missed mealtimes.

The heavens are not pouring wine
down the gullet of the city,
the streets are not littered
with cotton bowls of ambrosia.

Here is the reality:
other people's trash lying
as a testament to their morals,
weather-beaten and brown.

All the shutters are down,
on the bakeries, on the milk floats,
on the public bars
and on the people too.

# The Horses Are Eating Each Other

I hope this missive finds you
less insane than before, although
I have not one inkling as to what scale
sanity might be measured on these days.

I heard you've stopped screaming
into the void; good for you,
but occasionally you might whisper to it,
a child whispering to his monsters,
checking if they are still situated
in the same domain as their fear.

Your blue streak of paranoia
sealed my last letter to you
until finally a nurse, whether out of love
or vocational duty, decide to read it out;
although I fear she may have been liberal
in the translation, and inserted her own
ideas and empathy where evocation
let her down. Perhaps this was more a failure
in my own writings that her upbringing,
for you never can rely on someone having
just the right experiences to help
provoke just the right reaction.

Whether you listened with your heartbeat
picking out the cadence of my words
or sat there with a deaf mind,
I'm afraid my distance forbids me from knowing.

Forgive me for not using my blood as ink,
although I'm still not use if that is
an entirely unreasonable expectation.
Please know that I am yours sincerely,
if not always faithfully;
now hold my regards as you rock.

# I Wanna Be A Grown Up

Dear Winter,
I am writing to you
to apply for the position of icicle.

I realise there are already
many under your employment,
but figure that one more icicle
will not ruin the season.

I am tall and reasonably thin,
and can hang like a prosaic Egyptian statue,
arms and shoulders folded in,
legs crossed at the ankles;
if need be, I can lose weight
to be wiredrawn, and sprawling at over six feet,
I think I would be an excellent addition to your team.

At times, I can be cold and pointed in character,
and I'm sure if I concentrated, these traits
will transfer over to my physical demeanour.

One thing: once you are finished
with your annual cycle, could you see
that I am collected in some kind of receptacle
as I melt, and stored away until required the next year?

Yours in expectation,
Water.

# Into The Great Unknown

Shadows with lame feet
limp on Autumn floors;
only the unclasped concept of wind moves,
that physical phenomenon that feels non-physical,
unseen brushstrokes through the air:

like the love that apparently
comes from the heart
as if a pacemaker or a stent
or a double bypass
might harden that love;

such things we pretend to understand
and in that pretence, we get on with our lives,
filling bellies with refrigerated stars
and lining our eyes with crushed carbon coats
brought from the trove of manufactured dreams.

And into this, God's love,
the God who I cannot show you the beating heart of,
yet perhaps it is more important to look
not at the vessel, but rather
at the passengers instead.

# The Drawbridge Is Up

There is nothing in the news to arouse you
when you cannot consider the outer world;
another brick has been cemented in
with every new streaming headline.

The chisel of shock and awe
has become blunt under the inspection of
your great walls, Stonehenge in their magnitude,

but no soldiers are there to line your battlements;
the fortress lies like a granite ghost town,
the tumbleweeds toiling to gather momentum

as they plot their slow roll through your dust:
layered as security blankets may fall
across cowering children in an air-raid
waiting for the Blitz to pass.

# After You Go

After you go, there is the romantic debris
of dishes and tissues and empty CD cases,
tomes torn from the bookshelf
to confer with poems and the meaning of words
in the best of good-natured debate,
the mock arguments held with a smile.

After you go,
there are curled bed sheets to be straightened
transforming this double bed
into an oversized park bench for one;
the residual warmth of hugs and pillows
fading throughout the week until the next Friday arrives;
leftovers to be enjoyed as singular micro-meals.

After you go,
there is the silence of the empty dwelling,
the brick-held breath of one pausing
to survey his solitude, and finding companion
in memories and scattered mementos
lying as a mosaic of our time.

# The Jackpot Rush

It isn't the pram in the hallway
or the cot in what was once the spare room
that keeps us from achieving greatness.

Pens, swords, laurel leaves clutched
despairingly, triumphantly
in fist raised through victory or violence,

humanity subjecting itself
to its own potential for fallibility,
its potential to cradle the stars in the orphan night
and find greatness resting at its doorstep.

destined for eternity
to miss its chance at the jackpot:
a bitter husk
cutting its life down for fodder;
hostage to fortune, nepotism, old boy networks,
the wrong contacts;
cursing the time, the place,
the hour coming and finding no one willing
to take the reins and beat surrender.

Forget the haunt of the snow-ridden page
and press your footstep into
the whites of contemporary eyes,
overt with envy
at the achievement of others.

Trade in your crow for a starling,
a hawk for a blackbird,
and practice this literary falconry
just by being there:
breathe in life and milk out poetry
from the glands of desolate inspiration,
piling meat onto the tender, young bones
of skinny mongrels;
that experienced flesh
handed down from old thrones
and translated into
golden volumes of accomplishment.

A new king is crowned,
but great kings are never content.
Long live the King.

# Chasing

Old ladies at their fruit machines,
superstitions chasing jackpots
as the coffee and sandwiches fuel another hour.

Thin stream of gold
playing peek-a-boo around this crag,
small kiss, fickle minnow
undecided,
rainbow trout spinning hope,
such dumb, blind hope.

One could drown
in the collected tragedies of this room,
coloured lights deadening eyes and dreams.
Stroke your dragon's tooth,
the trouble of greed forever handicapping
any mournful reason.

# Rallentando

April's oppressive weight
is pressing into the crest of May,
stubborn, persistent knotweed
who will behead Spring and rail

against anterograde time.
His fingers fumbling to lock
around May's neck and thrust
her closer to the cliff edge.

This is not a flirt.
This is a threat,
real and calculated,
where only one flag can rise.

We know the end, having seen it
many times before; yet
out of feeble masochism,
always doubt the outcome.

# Xaviere

*After Simone de Beauvoir's She Came To Stay*

Xaviere, I have killed you many times over
and still you bleed for me.
I remember the full stop I left out at the end of the book,
and you came along to continue the sentence.
Finality was a fine illusion in those days;
back then, I thought we were finished.
Yet you carried our blood relationship on into closer bonds:
we became the double helix, the shoelaces intertwined,
the knots tightening on limpid skeletal limbs.
For a while, we were tame and passive towards each other;
now storm clouds pale in the shadows of our respective existences,
skies dancing around the sea of words and sounds
and tears and scars between us.
We may have been fools to continue,
but your bite was too strong
and my flesh too supple to resist.
I admit, when you left, I missed your inspiring embrace,
gold scaffolding around my broken bridges
and weather-torn brick hamlets.
Xaviere, I welcome you back into the dark,
I greet myself entering your glow;
we will never part again.

# Poem For October

I stepped off the bus and saw evening
in the reflection of the weather:
autumn cover settled in the rainfall
collected by pavement stones,
making me long for days watered down
by the evening spirit;
thoughts of travelling through Toome
and Randalstown at Christmas,
streetlight patterns filtered through windows,
daylight clinging onto the city streets
and battling around stonework and hall gates,
mixing brightness with celluloid dusk,
hitting the shoppers and hawkers alike.

October, and the night-time comes over
like a lover's blanket would be cast,
given up for shelter.
all I want now is to sleep,
an air of expectancy for rest.

# **Thoughts on an Unanswered Question**

Overheard in a yellowing bookstore:
"Did you get things thrown at you in school? No,
that's a silly question; people don't get
things thrown at them these days."

What curious universe is this?
Where confetti and bouquets lie dormant,
not to known the arc of celebration;
no stray pints of what you hope is festival beer;
the vacancy of rubbish strewn
from football crowds, tired party-goers.

The police rest well in this world,
without fear of stones and petrol bombs;
children never see a fist
or pages balled and lurched
towards bowed heads,
pointed paper planes
piercing the quietude.

No one is a target.
Our arms rest at our sides.

# Instant Thought

I will destroy
all the empty prophets
and self-declared legionnaires
of the flaccid newworldorder
pandering at the gates
of acceptance.

I will spit
in the eyes of the pissants
who write their epitaphs in chalk
but use the chisel on themselves
in order to be scarred-chic.

I will turn the gun away from myself
and target the vacuum,
netting charming charlatans in my scope
who are only willing
to publicise themselves.

They will not get my support anymore.
I will not add my water
to the freeze-dried, easy bake flippancies
they shit out of their pens,
expecting hero-worship as a reward
when they never get far enough from the toilet bowl
to raise a kingdom of their own.

# Press

Elemental forces fire across the vanguard,
single atoms of carbon, hydrogen,
oxygen, colliding and congealing together
in the loaded air found between synapses;
the blood sugar is running high,
worthy application of a hungry chi.

The printing press is ready to beat,
even if the weight behind the oil and soot
is not evenly submitted; the only matter
is the willing vellum, asking to be lit
by the fires of knowledge, its nature
to spread and consume the wicks of life.

Carve out the punches, build your frames
and set your lines: whether with genius
or steady practice and perfection,
or the predestined, noble hobble of time,
the potentials are there now to be clasped,
the sheaves dipped and diluted with force.

# Into Each Life Some Sun Must Shine

Today, the spirits are allowed to evade
on the proviso that they
are accompanied by the sun.

Summer has finally crawled its way
around the earth, found a path
out of the underworld

and nestled its yellow soul
at the edges of our skies;
the city working on its tan.

Let music play from the boroughs
and children shout out the hours;
my ears are lost in the placid hum

of warmth, of light, of simple miracles
such as one good day shining out
amid a season of blackitude.

# Swimming Around the Inkwell

I have known a few poets
who gave up
the good fight
and stopped writing.
They have not stopped altogether in life,
and have gone on to other
worthy applications
such as further education, unemployment
and generally getting on with things
instead of swimming around the inkwell
endlessly.

I say,
if the fight is truly good,
then you can never lose.

And it's a poor scrap of a losing battle
when each fist is a cliché,
with no blood left in your words.
Lost are the victories
of the Imagists, the Romantics,
the Lakes, the visionaries.
Instead, today,
we drown.

# Abandoned Teabag

There is a small teabag in the middle of the road,
abandoned, miles away from the warm resolve
of kitchen and kettle, now doomed to only feel rain
and never the welcoming splash of newly boiled water
promising to unlock its gluttony of flavour.
It is too damp, too worn to nestle in a mug;
to let its deathbed resemble its birth right.
Sorry, round white holder of foreign delights,
you may never be reborn, transformed
from dry creature into the swirling brown
sustenance of break time, of morning brew.
If only for a few glorious minutes, you had been
saved by the need for refreshment, now not even
feeling the stroke of a biscuit against your milky hide.

# Conditions for Prayer

Abandon the fireside, and instead
hush your eyes with reverent spirit.

Let the air be still around you,
and take in this placating stillness.

Dispense with pride, and adopt
the aged, bowed stance of humility.

Open your palms and feel anger as
water dropping from your pugilistic grasp.

Shed off claustrophobic layers
of retribution and resentment.

Let the spears in your flank dull
against the stone shield of resolve.

Hatred is a wasted motion
for the child who has not learnt fear.

# Drought

I rest in ploughed fields, waiting for rain,
that persistence absence
of a postnatal mother
not wanting to hold her child.

There is no fear of the embrace,
just disgust.

The soil permeates my skin,
a premature death of sorts,
preparing to land in ash and dust;
I am Prometheus in his death pit,
open to the floods.

# Hellos and Haloes

The soot gathers around my inglenook,
marking the statuettes I collected
from a lifetime of bumbled adventures.

I take the bellows to blow them clear,
instead of flexing my toneless arms
and kneeling into the crying fire.

Each coal-piece longs to say goodnight;
I goad them with recovered wood
and continue to eek out their exhaustion.

Damn, this room could use some air
but it's minus thirty-three out there
in Ireland's cruel airways.

Rather now, the walls become blackened,
brickwork coated with combusted evidence
accrued from too many winters alone.

And out the condensed window, I see
plumes arise from my neighbours' hearths,
waving possibilities of helloes and salvation.

# Graveside

The leaves have formed a mosaic across the lawn,
cracked tiles of decay looking for their return,
once emerald blanket now patchwork.

Trees have bent down to kiss the earth
and left their auburn lipstick behind,
ginger smudges blistering on greenery.

A season to be dying; mother branches struck bare
with grief, mourning their fallen children,
as Father Time decrees them all to be bastards.

He condemns them to death, the trees standing
as womenfolk around the open grave,
already feeling germination in their bellies.

# Hold

The music does not hold the right notes;
the sun has lost its hold on the sky;
this bed holds too much of my time.

The unsteady cadence of my days
tick against battered percussion,
skins beaten by tree trunks,
where even steel crumples
in opposition to this song.

I'll close my eyes and hum
a trick of enforcement:
no ancient *om* or enchanted tone
pitched at the world's orchestra;
just the open palm and upright spine
measured alongside the curve
of modernity, the stable breath
in contrast to every motor
and throat screaming outside
the window, whose harsh vibrations
spoil my enjoyment of the air.

# Strangled

I want to tear down the fences
and instead plant stems of ladders,
with binoculars for flower-heads,
so I can at last see my homeland
pass the distance of unknowing.

I want to cut through the wire
instead of its reality cutting me;
perimeter of skin diminishing each day,
eyes sinking into darkness,
the sun, an alarm from Hell.

I want to pile up the bodies
instead of hushing up the truth,
build a black tower of testimony:
here is my heritage, blistered by hatred,
my youth, butchered by death's brand.

# Outran

The clouds wall over us
but we were never promised sun;
that's dismissed as foolish optimism.

We have our accessories for the season.
warmth of cloth as our first skin proves lacking.
I'm only muscle and bone; it's no contest.
The wind runs faster, rain falls quicker
then we can step;
we who have the nature of risk,
of gamble, win or loss:
us who must go on despite everything
while the storm just is and will be
regardless of our tiny shelters.

We're livestock hedged into our fields.
Whatever reason or intentions
we may throw upwards,
the sky knows not of mercy.

# Affective

The box encloses,
six sides of Autumn
snuffing out the light of your summers.

Punch a hole in the wall
and force a crack;
stick your fingers in
and tease the space, find
brick and mortar malleable
to your touch; widen the hole
and insert a window where your fist laid.

Open that window
and let the air moisturise your thoughts;

and then, when no one's looking,
crawl through the frame
and escape into
the unknown.

# ACKNOWLEDGEMENTS:

Thank you to the editors of the following journals and anthologies in which these poems originally appeared (some in a slightly different form):

Alors, et Toi?, A New Ulster, amphibi.us, Bareback Magazine, BBC Get Writing Northern Ireland, blue & yellow dog, The Blue Nib, Black Mountain Review, Boyne Berries, Calliope Nerve, Community Arts Partnership, ctrl+alt+del, Eclectic Eel, Elohi Gadugi, etcetera, Extract(s), Fire, The First Cut, FourXFour, Gutter Eloquence, Illuminated Poetry Ireland, Incandescent Poetry, Keep Her Lit, Literary Chaos, Message In A Bottle Poetry, Negative Suck, Oddball Magazine, Open City 360, Poetry Super Highway, Prairie Schooner, The Pygmy Giant, The Ranfurly Review, Red Pulp Underground, Revival, Right Hand Pointing, riverbabble, Solstice Initiative, Stimulus Respond, The Survivor's Guide to Bedlam, Tripping on Words: A Literary Atlas, Unquiet Desperation, weasel & gun, Why Vandalism?, Wordlegs and Zygote Abstract.

*Perhaps* was the winner of the Edit Red Writers' Choice Award for Poetry, 2006.

*The Stare Across the Room* was part of 'James Barrett and the Doll in the Corner' exhibition by Kathy Marsh, August 2000.

*Flagging* was displayed in Belfast Central Library as part of their World Poetry Day Celebrations, March 2014.

*Outran* was displayed at part of North West Words' Poetry For Space Project, April 2013.